BUOYANCY CONTROL

BUOYANCY CONTROL

Adrienne Gruber

BookThug 2016

FIRST EDITION
copyright © 2016 by Adrienne Gruber

ALL RIGHTS RESERVED

No part of this publication may be reproduced or transmitted in any form or by any means, electronic or mechanical, including photocopying, recording, or any information storage or retrieval system, without permission in writing from the publisher.

The production of this book was made possible through the generous assistance of the Canada Council for the Arts and the Ontario Arts Council. BookThug also acknowledges the support of the Government of Canada through the Canada Book Fund and the Government of Ontario through the Ontario Book Publishing Tax Credit and the Ontario Book Fund.

LIBRARY AND ARCHIVES CANADA
CATALOGUING IN PUBLICATION

Gruber, Adrienne, 1980–, author
    Buoyancy control / Adrienne Gruber. —First edition.

Poems.
Issued in print and electronic formats.
ISBN 978-1-77166-222-2 (PAPERBACK)
ISBN 978-1-77166-223-9 (HTML)
ISBN 978-1-77166-224-6 (PDF)
ISBN 978-1-77166-225-3 (MOBI)

    I. Title.

PS8613.R79B86 2016   C811'.6   C2016-900582-8
                                          C2016-900583-6

PRINTED IN CANADA

For Edith and Salvador, pa que sepas.

CONTENTS

TERRA FIRMA

A MARI USQUE AD MARIA

PROLOGUE

Blend of heat and colour. Bougainvillea bloom in January, cacti buds are sunsets. Scrub dishes, stoke the fire, bring in wood, play a game of dominoes, help Salvador wash his car. Walk in the groves with the dogs, throw them pieces of orange. Occupy restless hands. Salvador makes perfume. Fingers measure and pour the alcohol. The bottles smell like candy. Twice a week the shrill siren of a tortilla truck passes through El Llano. Dogs have flies around their mouths. Women in television commercials are whiter than you are. Learn to say *café con leche*; this is what a woman's skin looks like. Think of a man once loved, planned a life with. Bike down a gravel switchback, launch head first over the handlebars. The bike on top, the sun, a frying pan branded to back. On Saturdays, the market in Montemorelos. Boiled corn mixed with salsa and *crema fresca*. Kids sell toy cars and Spiderman dolls, cowboy belt buckles. Silver purses and pink lipsticks. A scruffy one-eared dog trots by, nipples dragging like udders. Whoever sucks her dry gets a mouthful of dust. Fifty-cent bottles of beer are sweeter than milk. A man lifts iron birdcages out of a truck, glint of green-tipped wings—*palomas*; their muffled throated coos. At the market, look for a mortar and pestle to grind chilies. On New Year's Eve in Monterrey, eat pale cow intestines in gunpowder broth. Shots are heard all evening; children set off firecrackers and twirl sparklers. The neighbours play mariachi until six a.m. A car alarm runs for hours before the battery gives out. Even in rain, no decisions are made. The dogs stay inside, except the ones at the baseball field, digging through wet leaves at the foot of the bleachers. Leave a beer bottle on the pitcher's mound, a bundle of roadside azaleas. Back at the house, cookbooks exasperate. No recipe for meatloaf. The rain pounding on the roof is worse than the hail of pecans let loose by the night wind. The cold and its contagion. Water moves toward a bed of cement into a pool, the way mercury slides along kitchen tile, thermometer in shards. Stick hands in the meat, raw and slippery. Lupita, next door, calls *Adrianna* and gives little cakes to take home. Enrique's roosters claw the dirt. Always a cockroach beside the shoes, an exoskeleton. In the kitchen, a fire in a small dark corner. Hold hands over until they blister. Outside the dogs carry oranges like softballs in their mouths. There isn't anything to do but pass the time. Dangle feet in the irrigation water. Bougainvillea, hibiscus, buttered sunflowers. Dogs follow to the river. One finds a turtle and bats it around. I can't hold on to anything.

TERRA FIRMA

THE HANGED WOMAN

1.

If Tarot were to read itself while driving through Kansas,
boxes crammed to the roof, salt streaking the car,
it would turn up the hanged woman.
Indecision. Twelfth trump card.
The traitor. I need a clear road scraped of debris.
The sun doctors the land pristine, like the white gold
on mother's wedding band, or the sugar bowl
with its blueberry handle. Even clichés of bone
or glass are less predictable in this light. Their protrusions shrill
as teeth. My friend says she believes in the sublime
as a religion. The word muddy on the brain as we make
the drive south. She speaks of mercury molecules, the split
of threaded cells that fall to the floor, skim the linoleum
as silver balls. The highway glimmers. Soon we'll cross
the border.

2.

Sunday in Nebraska there's nothing on the radio
but Jesus. The sun against snow is blinding. Every sin
is sexual. Child sings off-key about the morning star.
Banjos and mandolins play Handel's Messiah. At the Rockport
gas station you can buy Betty Boop alarm clocks, snow globes
holding churches. In Nebraska every gas station is proud
of its kitsch. A room at the end of the hall is filled
with dolls and blank stares. Toddlers with fuchsia cheeks,
missing pupils, white curls. One sleeps
on her side, goldfish lips, pink eyelids and
half-closed mouth. A still, open shell.

3.

Cross the border
at three a.m. Mother refuses to leave the car,
protects my sister's wedding dress.
Everywhere babies and cars with furniture
tied to the roof. First glimpse of Mexico.
Circling the gates, searching for the way in.

Drive through Monterrey early morning
streets slick. Dad strains his eyes. Location signs lie.
80 km to El Llano, then 94 km.

Pick an orange at sunrise when the stars are bright.
Suckle the fruit.
Juice slips from lips as sweat gathers
at the small of my back.

4.

bellinis   the tiny windows on planes   her lips
on the dance floor   jellyfish acid grip
stench of old pennies   pulling into the ditch
to masturbate
the small blond boy who eats rice and beans
while watching Ms. Packman   a seahorse
liquid that breaks and gushes as amniotic fluid   swell
of the tide   when a puffer fish is troubled   a hand
on your thigh   the streets between two and four a.m.   balconies
rain surging from the sky   old typewriters   habits
that should break   the word lynx   the Neptune fountain
at the Macro Plaza in Monterrey   the marbled woman
water glazing her breasts

5.

Each grain of sand is the earth
if you let it. What hatches in your palm
without knowing. The leather seats
bake your groin. Drive into the city where
tar melts the streets. Stop at Tortas Alex
for a sandwich. A sticky ball of baby
spiders nests against your corduroy purse.
They spill onto your lap and spring into the world
writhe against your thighs. You jump
from the car, swear, swipe at your crotch.
Bodies fly in all directions.

PROPOSAL

      Let's make babies, something solid that slips
with its own mucus trap, screaming at the world
betrayal with its first breath. This has nothing to do
with love. It's basic sorcery. What you can do for me.
We climb out of caskets
once sawed in half. Birth magicians

      like breath.
Like the sticky remains
on the Trans-Canada, the deer whose legs
I ran over in the middle of the night. The substance
we are after, all colour, a freshly painted room

      where the smell silences those first few brain cells.
A man pushes two fingers inside me and groans.
The liquid phase. You taste tart, he says and lowers
his mouth.
Remember the truck stop cherry pie
I ate the night we couldn't get to Oklahoma.
The quiver of fruit
membrane on my tongue; how a jellyfish dissolves
on hot sand. Think of the baby

      who thrust out, the placenta
its inverted twin. Think of my mother
who couldn't hold her bowels as she pushed
out my sister, the nurse trying to convince her,
pressure in the uterus. And what he moans
in my ear, trying to reach deeper.
A canker in the mouth,
a dark hair wisping from the breast.

A dark hair wisping from the breast.
A canker in the mouth.
In my ear, trying to reach deeper,
pressure in the uterus. And what he moans
out. My sister—the nurse trying to convince her—
who couldn't hold her bowels as she pushed
its inverted twin. Think of my mother
        who thrust out the placenta

on hot sand. Think of the baby
membrane on my tongue; how a jellyfish dissolves.
The quiver of fruit
I ate the night we couldn't get to Oklahoma.
Remember the truck stop cherry pie,
his mouth.
The liquid phase. You taste tart, he says and lowers.
A man pushes two fingers inside me and groans,
        where the smell silences those first few brain cells.

We are, after all, colour. A freshly painted room.
I ran over, in the middle of the night, the substance
on the Trans-Canada. The deer whose legs
like the sticky remains –
        like breath

once sawed in half. Birth magicians.
We climb into caskets
with love, its basic sorcery. What you can do for me.
Betrayal with its first breath. This has nothing to do
with its own mucus trap screaming at the world.
        Let's make babies. Something solid. That slips.

THE WORLD, DIVIDED

A shell finds you when cleaning out the pack
at the end of a trip to Playa del Carmen. Ascend

from the ocean floor, drag everything up
with you, let it dry in the sun. The endoskeleton

hammered into rock by the snarl of a wave.
We are considered complete

on our own.
There are separate stalls

in the restaurant bathroom, twin
rolls of toilet paper. Double-ply. Matching sinks and

mirrors. You see both of yourself.
Slice the cavity into duets, divide

the leftover organs.
Only the heart sits in its solitary sac.

You couldn't get onto the ark
without her.

THE SUMMER I WAS HER HEDONIST

One night she is determined to photograph me naked, guttural.
Her cabin at the acreage, spread-eagled in her hatchback, kneeling
behind the driver's seat, aperture sealed between thighs.
Diffuse. Shudder. The mirror opens; exposure. Our shadows
stilted. The syntax of my back slack-shift, off-kilter. The double helix
of our mating. We produce nothing
but the stick of the shutter. The blue-black filter of night licks
the dim tungsten bulb that burns against the nervous corner.
Would these photos tell us more about ourselves? Kaleidoscope-bound
contortionists. The dream of us furrows its way into night.

EVER AFTER

Our wedding day should be full of butterflies:
fossorial apprentices to the sky. The best man
holds the glass lid tight over the sleeping,
sunken eyes. The twisted breeze.
The sun huddles, pigmented. Ignites strappy shoes,
garments, the electricity of damp thighs.
The crowd hungers and assembles.
The lid opens; prism-scaled wings,
large batting eyelashes crumple to the ground.
Half-dead and drunk on dying.

THE SUMMER I PLAYED WITH POLY

I feared confrontation.
Eggs whipped at the panes of front windows,
up the ladder to chisel them off in
August fever. A martini in the face, ice-blue
run off, mouthwash sting sticky
condensation of breath. Or simply
tears that flow like glacial melt where, as kids,
we'd place our warm sodas to cool.
But she didn't know and for that
I was grateful. I was kicking the stars with both feet
leaving my purse on her car as we drove out of town.
The fisherman's wife returned it the next day
the leather glued together from the Sunday sun
a peacock tail of feathered eye shadow dripping
like extra paste on a schoolboy's collage.
It sticks to the table when the teacher comes
to inspect just as her parents came
and we bolted, eight a.m.,
the heat already unbearable.

THE PLANETS NEVER ALIGN FOR YOU

the more furious the star, the brighter it burns
—David Hickey

How furious you are
with your heart and the sheer will of it
to hold tight the crux
of capillary function, the dank scent of iron,
the dark that never left. Pump away.
The hidden spool of arteries foil
even the best of us. The fossil corked
from the chest. You have never felt betrayed
quite like this. The head of a mollusk pokes out
from the husk of longing. There's no shame
in forgiveness. Enough pillow talk. You are here
and the day burns brighter for it. The fist
clenched, pudgy organ just as furious.
Mince arguments into a Möbius strip.
The moist socked-feet of moving on. Contempt grilled
on the barbeque, black-market thoughts;
shucking organs for soup. How punctured
your breath. Survey the space
where your lover's furniture once lay,
those chalk outlines where the dog huddles.
A headache in the airport bar
next to the woman who eats tuna out of the can.
Insomnia tonight, rebellion tomorrow.
Pulling teeth. And still, they insist,
the heart is the measure of success.

ONLY HE KNOWS THE STORY OF
HIS PRECIOUS AND PARTICULAR LIFE

An intruder, I watch you down at the edge,
toes curl around rough planks, knees bend
then straighten, fists on hips, a dip
of one toe in the frigid mouth. I could butt out this cigarette,
drink a bourbon, draw an s o s in the dirt
in the time it takes to make up your mind.
The jump must be done without thinking. Before the brain
takes over and compensates for pain
or wracked conscience. Smoke gathers
into lungs with one collapsible breath. Wind rushes
through your ears and upsets the balancing act
this tiptoe riot.

The cracks in the two-by-fours fade
from the sun's filtration, the gait of the fractured
wind splits knobs in the wood. My toes mimic
your toes. Your knees flex,
half-bowed to an audience of duck shit splattered
on the dive plank. Power's out.
Inside the cottage, ice cream floods
the freezer. You and, consequently, I
are stuck. The fold and bend of
your gargoyled shadow bisects my heart.
The light, spliced with cloud, injures us with
a glib fondle of hope. I bring you to life.
Unsuspecting marionette. The strings in my hands
paper-thin (tug once, twice). Your arms levitate.
The tightness in your neck. Pull back. Release.

I understand. The time I flung myself down the wooden steps
at Eagle Lake I lost footing or footing lost me, face down
on the dock, knees scraped and half a toenail cockeyed.
Later, I jumped in the body and swam the length of it
algae-soaked cryptids nibbling my ankles.
I could comprehend drowning. My frog kick quickened.
The past is an undertow. Even the dock spiders couldn't keep me
from scrambling back up the ladder. In the here-and-now
I can shift molecules, sever cells. I can bully
the strain in your calves to collapse. Stop examining
your sunned chest, the coils of dark hair.
Stop wiping the sweat from your brow.

Stars fixate on blackened water. Nails dig
scabs of mosquito scarring. Meanwhile, you exist,
unaware that I have never found you
more beautiful. Spark-plugged limbs
meat of dry mouth. The past is an undertow;
we do not know how we got here.
Your simple bum, tight in train-conductor trunks.
The strain of this balancing act, each of us
worthy of that beauty somehow.

FLASH FLOOD

The pizza comes in triangles.
Each wedge with minced garlic and olives.
We sprawl the bed in holey underwear.
Cheese strings stretch from our lips.
Unabashedly human.
The bath fills with untamed fluid.
Razor in one hand.
Frothy brush in the other.
He lingers.
Coarse ringlets wash up against inlet groin.
High tide weeps.
Sweeps dead things to shore.
Roll my body over.
Note the rise of my bum
The camber of back.
Splash of awkward shape.
Towel dry my delicates.
The bed stains with the cleanest skin.
I sink deep and dark and bloated with heat.
His face between my limbs.
Performed burial.
Strength steams in when least expected.
Water surges down my thighs.
I let my breath out for the first time.

MIMIC

The Indonesian mimic octopus, Thaumoctopus mimicus, is a species of octopus that has a strong ability to mimic other creatures. It grows up to 60 cm (2 feet) in length. Its normal colouring consists of brown and white stripes or spots. Living in the tropical seas of Southeast Asia, it was not discovered officially until 1998, off the coast of Sulawesi. The octopus mimics the physical likeness and movements of more than fifteen different species, including sea snakes, lionfish, flatfish, brittle stars, giant crabs, sea shells, stingrays, flounders, jellyfish, sea anemones, and mantis shrimp. It accomplishes this by contorting its body and arms, and changing colour.

—Wikipedia, 2010

CIRCUS

In a house of mirrors a zebra-streaked mollusk stretches like the Big Top.
All the children flock to your stripes, desire candy floss, the trapeze man. Carnies step aside, their gritty lungs cough obscenities as all the women gather to watch you change shape before their eyes. Waving two arms like white flags you whisk along the silted bottom. Flirt with the damselfish in distress. All eight of your arms meant for lovemaking.

THE FREAK SHOW

I regenerate lost limbs.
Actual or metaphorical, amputate

myself—take what you will;
what's left behind

will grow another animal.
I carry an invisible set of spikes

along my spine. Hard-caked
calluses on my underside.

A retractable heart. I'll leave
an appendage behind if need be.

I've got resources.
I'm just saying.

THE SIDESHOW

Watching you on the patio
drill holes into our bed frame,

tentacles wrap around the windowsill
suction onto glass, my beak

bone-hard. You stain two-by-fours, curse
the bruise of rain clouds. My true form threatens

to betray. Cluster of fishhooks
suckle the imitation flesh out of me. I bang

into foreign objects, barriers, a landfill
of your objections and desires.

THE AFTER SHOW

We drag the futon mattress into the living room
and I read to you. *Peace at Last*, the book

my mother used to read at bedtime.
I do the voices,

then agitate the duvet and hide beneath it.
You've become fluent

in sleep. No buzzing fan or growl
of restless cats to burden you.

I am flattened stiff in our bed.
Thick cartilage of vigil.

FIGHTING PRESERVATION IS HARLEQUIN

hours past dawn and I fake sleep   lack-lustre avoidance
of your morning rigamarole   tongue on tongue

                         water to fuse my lungs

a placenta stuck to the wall of the sea
stiff flecked polyp

                         the hollow heart in
                         disguise

sticky pickle jar of ocean   my love
harpooned   sweet and oozing   my cavity

                         is your cavity darling

this body we share   curved moon sickle
tenuous space that dissipates

                         this melancholy
                         stench of longing

you and I planting roots
stake into ground

                         how Darwinian of us

how we attach is umbilical
tentacle

our skins uncovering

I'll buy the eggs and milk   you wheel the suitcase
full of dirty laundry down the street

WE ARE CONSIDERED COMPLETE ON OUR OWN

In spite of the temptation to perform a disappearing act
    or use your eight arms

to impersonate Jesus, the show must go on. There is no
    slamming door temper-tantrum defeat

no climbing down from the balcony after a
    pseudo-romanticized declaration

of love. Our apartment stands solid
    in its crumbled foundation,

sprinkle of decay, stain and lacquer. Cubed rooms
    with our belongings. Smatter

of tiny water balloons explode on showering bodies,
    race down backs like bile. We slip under—

mass of greedy pincers. We move lazily—
    the drippings of pancake batter.

Take inventory: the jaundiced bed lamp, collection
    of cat-litter crumbs; our

stalemate affections. There is mimicry in sleep.
    You toss at my turn.

PROLOGUE

I hobble gingerly along stones to the second beach at Lake Superior.
Fossilized imprints sketch the bottoms of my feet into Rorschachs.
The tide's pulse soothes a cluster of rock formations.
Here, I lay myself down.

Warm breath against naked gleam.
Flutter in my vulva. Groin oscillates.
Lonely sun pounds against shoulders.
I am ridged with contusions.

My fingers are beach hoppers. Skitter and quarry.
Glacial flood baptizes my goose hair.
The new world rushes in.
I peed when I came. Everything water.

A MARI USQUE AD MARIA

OYSTER

Drink it slow, says the girl who takes you
on her Vespa along the freeways of Manhattan, who dresses
all in black, face a sharp-eyed cat. Oyster juice
dribbles down her chin and she catches it with a napkin. *Can you
taste it?* she asks, and you nod, not at all sure what she means.
The ocean, she says. *Now close your eyes,* and you do.
Sip the salty water, granules of the shell roll around
in your mouth. Nibble the oyster like touching tongues.
Open your eyes. She tilts her head back and pours the fleshy
meat down her throat. A bathtub made of marble, legs stretched
in lukewarm, the girl sprawled against your solid frame. It is this
and every image like it that prevents you from moving forward.
You take a cautious bite, pulp against your teeth. The summer
in Tofino, the afternoon at Long Beach, your face dry and sunburnt.
Find shells and smell their insides. Musky. The girl's eyes watch
your mouth as you chew small plump bites. You can't bear
to swallow something so raw, so full of life.

DICKIE LAKE 1

Launch upright, slip into the water.
Murky drink tongues the edges of doubt.

A held breath, swirl of milky clarity. The remainder
of days are lonely as a motel ship painting.

Sky stretches; the toffee-flux of time.
Heart jeers; queer as a French Horn.

Moon billows and purges light, a shroud. The roundness
of full-figured flesh against gloomy trunks.

I pull myself out. Plunk these dumb feet
into the lake. Wet back smacks against rough boards,

thighs fissured. The words will come
spit-shined and polished.

KLAUS RICARDO

Sister (swathed in damp towels, flailing brat, sour-tempered beast) pushes away all hands. Coerces Mum for pots of hot water, warm milk with honey. Swallows crusts of cold toast while forehead secretes. Scrambles from standing to squatting to down-on-all-fours. Glazed eyelids droop in sullen defiance.

Just three hours, eight hours, eleven hours earlier she plucks chile pequins from dried bushes. Pilfers limes under an aching sun; one hand lazy on her bulge. Between thrashing and sleep, Sister longs for a Russian water birth. Women with sexy contracted moans. Toddlers bounce like dumplings in bloody baths, finger the spongy suckling crown.

Sister claws the headboard, hair strung in spools. Imagines herself a molting snake. Swore she would not scream, but her cries are turbulent, louder than grief, than the groan of cervix. An audience of cocked spines rock anxiously to the orchestra. Tepid coffee between sharp, atomized shrieks. Outside, a cow wails.

This slippery sunken treasure, this niño, this place between silence and screams. Come. This murky swamp, this lover's hand against Sister's damp neck. Come. Condensation hangs as indecision in the air. Come. Pale glow of morning peaks her defeated shoulders. Come. *All thought blasted into the night sky.*

THE SUMMER I CAPSIZED YOU

A Dolly Parton remix or the moisture of club sweat or bodies unsteady under disco lighting. The beer loosens limbs. Bump up against queens and dykes, twinks making out with vigour; one pulls his shirt off, reveals a hoop harnessing a doughy nipple.

A documentary about forest kindergarten in Switzerland plays while we fool ourselves on the couch. An old doll's appendage digs into my spine. Her hair froths wild. She pulls us both into the bedroom.

My body capsized. The raft hardly big enough for two.

The waves roll in. The shoreline is a fixed point. We wash up drenched, salt-sputtering. Heave our bodies onto dry land. *I've never shivered and convulsed as hard in my life.*

THE SWIMMER VIGNETTES

> *You can tell a lot about a person from seeing them in the water.*
> —Lidia Yuknavitch

1.

Just like Mother, I threw myself
in the coldest lakes and rivers. Unafraid, we'd languish
in hypothermia, surface with goose pimples and smirks.
Sister, a smaller, paler version of me, dark hair, stick legs,
inched her way into that rush of liquid ice
the way one approaches the mouth of a cave.
It took an hour to make it to her belly button.
She'd scoop handfuls against her white thighs
grimace at the assault on skin.

2.

The first time we swam together you became an eight-year-old boy.
Demeanor once calm, business-like, your body threw itself again
into the surge, limbs akimbo. A disturbance approached and
all the children fled to their mothers. I hovered at the shoreline
snapping stills as white foam submerged my toes.
The murky sky churned my hair, blended drink of brine and
surf and bedraggled weeds woven from sea clutches. You emerged
garrulous, victorious as though you'd run a marathon. Your load
lightened. The shame deep in your obese belly
the calm before the storm.

3.

He is birthed in the blue plastic pool.
A born swimmer. The harbour forgotten.

4.

Your face like a clown, laughter
between my legs. It only takes two
inches of water to drown.

5.

Under our smiles, fear.
If only water didn't equal loss.
Our awkward limbs.
No gills. No fins.

DICKIE LAKE 2

The curtains spread, breach
of flesh. The black room. Crisp debris

of barbequed yams. Light flickers
from a half-dead bulb.

Dirty pond browning in the sink.
The sinkhole in the dark

is this cleft of hip.
Count ribs with a drift of index finger.

Sheets flap in the wind,
orchestra of brass and strings.

Everything moans
reproduction. Unending

creation. Juggernaut.
Arrest my fingers.

Spread wide and deep.
The cellist runs the bow

along pelvis. Horsehair
gentle against thighs.

Outside the canoe thrashes.
Spasms from the scent of lake.

THE NEAR-DEATH EXPERIENCES YOU INEVITABLY HEAR WHILE LEARNING HOW TO DIVE

Mike's best friend takes his new weight belt diving
at Whytecliff and finds himself in an uncontrolled descent—
claws the rock wall, jaw clicks side to side.
Vision distorted. Static rises in his chest
as white noise fills the pockets between his teeth.
He pulls the quick release on his belt and propels up,
lungs full of ground glass.

You may find, in an emergency situation,
you must drop your weights.

All Mike says to me is *watch out*
for bursting lungs. He has a talent
for increasing my paranoia.
He's an opera singer,
what does he know about lungs?

THERE ARE TIMES WHEN GRAVITY COMES IN HANDY

We sink a little before we float, says Bernie. No kidding. Choke on my first breath. Bodies float among square tiles. Chlorine at the back of my throat. Air enters lungs through a tube. The guy with the tiki shorts and shaved chest is doing fine. Asshole. I swam before I could walk. Thigh-deep in Lake Superior, water lapped my diaper as I gnawed on an iceberg. My family played Frisbee on the shore. It was November. Water's my thing. Bernie claps his hands. Two fingers to his eyes. His mask is off, hair sways above his head. He's known people to vomit into their regulators. Swallowing must be okay. Ignore my arms, uncontrollable tentacles, useless in the management of technology. Resistant against the regulator. Try not to notice the agility of those around me. The movie I watched in high school: Men and women floating around the aircraft eating space food. A man peels a banana, twirls it and lets go. It spirals across the cabin and into a woman's mouth. I'm sure when the lights are off he unzips his spacesuit. With one hand cupped, twirls his body until he reaches the woman. He only has one shot.

OPEN WATER

As though blown up from the tail,
a puffer inflates. Water fills
the elasticity of his stomach. Eyes bulge,
pectoral fins frantic. Lower teeth jut.
There are no mollusks to gouge.
His two-chambered heart pumps
bloody terror. There must be
a hand to take. A pair of eyes to
lock with.

BUOYANCY CONTROL

> *Studies show your demographic does well to take up hobbies.*
> —Karen Solie

Deflate. Weighted hips allow you to sink.
Bubbles rise to the surface. Descent is an act

of control. Swallow. Move through metres of water
and calculate. Swallow again. Stop here. Pinch your nose.

A forced drowning. Fins erect. *I am not a fish. I am
not equipped.* Jaw jiggle. It's unnatural—

canned air. Drift up a few feet and settle. The birth
of each breath is recycled. Dead air finds its way

through clefts in the lungs. The evidence trapped—bubble
in the brain. Below, surface direction is lost.

The drone of a motor occupies the space where gravity remains
a trick question. Don't ask. Instead, note your surroundings.

Clear the mask and sing a stream of bubbles to the sky.
The instrument used to stay alive constricts

your lungs. Swallow. Recycled air. Claustrophobic
haze. Think possibilities. Running out of breath, gloom

behind your eyes. You are hugged by equipment.
This is all the love anyone needs.

RESCUE

> *A 46-year-old Port Moody woman was on life support in Vancouver General Hospital Sunday night after a scuba diving accident at Whytecliff Park in West Vancouver. Sgt. Paul Skelton said police got a call at noon Sunday, after a female diver failed to surface while on a dive with her partner at the popular scuba diving spot near Horseshoe Bay.*
> —ScubaBoard, Aug 23, 2010

You come to rest in a swell of Plumose.
Lungs are a tricky business.
Before this, you surfaced
once, twice.

            thrash of boots and blur of hand
            fingertips outstretched albino starfish
            his gold wedding band glints in
            the sun

The motor frantic overhead.
Corkscrew through the sinus cavity.
A jungle of nerves.

            the air between screams pounding
            echo of pulse shredded remains of
            jellyfish from a motorboat and after
            the gulls

Your brain grows dumber. Sometimes shells
are just shells; their spirals no longer
an infinite. There's no prophecy
under this liquid ceiling.

                sunlight streams through water
                face a contorted panic feral growl
                ocean and spit-filled mouth

A gas leak. Your five-year-old's missing
tooth, a gap in his smile. Your eight-year-old
keeps three in the battery compartment
of her digital camera. She rattles it to hear
the clinking of battered and broken teeth.

                caviar pop of fluid mosquito bites
                chicken pox nipples dipped into
                hungry mouths bubbles float lazily
                from lips

The Plumose gardens aren't as beautiful
as the last time. The visibility is bad.
The cauliflower plants are grey and sickly.
You stroke the spaghetti-shaped animal.
This is not good diver etiquette.
It will be fifteen minutes before they find your body.

grief thumbs his eyes blind
uncompromising the stilted measure
of goodness blue sky and stillness
mirrors that stretch and elongate the
face her slippery hand through his
the sun shines the gulls are lazy
everything is the same

FLUIDITY

In the end there is only swallowing and inhalation.
Two dichotomous acts that move things deep into us,
debilitate or free us dependant on reflex and
how steadily the heart pumps.

INTERTIDAL ZONES

"This filthy anemone, which exhibits both male and female characteristics, is turning our oceans' intertidal zones into dens of sin and perversion," said Rev. William Chester, spokesman for the Save Our Seas Coalition, a Huntsville-based activist group dedicated to 'the preservation of aquatic decency and morality.' "For God knows how long, this twisted sea creature has been running rampant in our oceans, spreading its unnatural, bisexual lifestyle. And it's high time somebody took a stand."

—"Transgendered Sea Anemone Denounced As 'Abomination' By Clergy," *The Onion*

REASONS TO CHOOSE THE SEA ANEMONE AS YOUR LOVER

I am that filth, a twisted creature. I loved the anemone of her, that five-fingered pulsing dance. I pack, strapped and fully loaded. Float amiss in intertidal zones, search for the slag that could match mine. A predatory flower. Large polyps digest prey. I could use a bit of digesting myself. With fifty or five hundred fingers, I am my own lover. Get myself off, wet an ocean's worth. Your shape indicates an attraction to kink. Egg and sperm eject through the mouth. Buds separate into two halves, a twinned life. Size is not a factor: four millimetres and eight thousand nerve endings can't be wrong.

AND REASONS NOT TO

How long have I hovered open-mouthed, weeping? For years I lived a half-life. Wait for the love of a good woman, then mope for the cock of a good man. How do we fold within ourselves and come out whole? Pick a side, for tits' sake. Give me penetration; separate the conjoined sexes and bring them to their knees. Lecherous love be damned.

REASONS TO CHOOSE THE LEAFY SEA DRAGON AS YOUR LOVER

Narrated by Jim Carrey, you were featured in a slow-motion 3D IMAX. Relative of the seahorse—same delicate trumpet nose, same philosophy of child rearing. Found in shallow pools, spindly figure hovers over brown kelp beds. Scales umbilical in texture. Titanium sheath. Mr. Nice Guy. Not like the Spanish Dancer, her large gelatinous figure used to her advantage. My love, you float up and down like a teeter-totter. Leaf-stalk fins plush as feathers stroke the side of my face. Not everything is meant to move in this way. The sea urchin suctions itself to the floor. The cucumber wraps its toothy meat around a soggy log. Hunting is patience. Panting, silence and heat.

AND REASONS NOT TO

Not nearly as exciting as the Indonesian Mimic Octopus. Limited mobility. 'Making love' is boring.

REASONS TO CHOOSE THE STARFISH
AS YOUR LOVER

The starfish is brought home in a Ziploc baggie, a purple bruise splayed stiff, withered from lack of moisture. The jellyfish dilutes overnight, but the starfish sits taut on the toilet frame for years. It does not yield. On the floor of Howe Sound they pile on top of each other, desperate for a feeding, a sheltered spot for regeneration. I read once that *all stars are fires, but not all fires are stars*. The burgundy hibiscus opens itself towards you with its five points. Hold it in your palm. All things take the same shape if you look closely. Some stars exist without oxygen or gravitational pull. Others inhale through submersion, their five or fifty legs rough tongues along the ocean floor.

REASONS TO CHOOSE THE JELLYFISH
AS YOUR LOVER

Folds. Plasm. Discharge along my thigh.
Black-lit. Backlit. Electricity trails in blooms.
Consistency. Repetition. Pulse. Pulse.   Pulse.

AND REASONS NOT TO

> *...perhaps the jellyfish understands, in ways that we cannot, that everything must tend toward liquid.*
>
> —BH

Our last day of vacation and the sand is so hot we limp along its surface. I am full of salt grime reaching to my pubis, my chapped inner thighs. A wave dissolves my calf. A stiff bubble corkscrews along my leg abstract until the searing heat reaches my brain. It's only a rope, you say, ripping its bulbous head from my limb. We have ways to dispose of what tends to liquid. We have the ocean, where all things gather, where all things dispel. How can we explain the jellyfish that washes up on shore, sticks to flesh but is not meant to hold on for a lifetime? We have no choice but to fling these boils back into the sea. Our clutch is too tight, our desire too great.

REASONS TO CHOOSE THE GLAUCUS AS YOUR LOVER

Because it is known as the sea swallow blue angel blue glaucus blue dragon blue sea slug blue ocean slug and when you take away the blues and the seas and the ocean you are left with swallow angel glaucus dragon slug.

AND REASONS NOT TO

You are the real live Pokémon. Pocket monster.

REASONS TO CHOOSE THE SEAHORSE AS YOUR LOVER

You mate for life. Range in size from 0.6-14 inches long and, at best, hover without the ability to swim or defend yourself. With little chance of survival, you choose to celebrate life. A love-making ritual lasts nine hours. You shift like a mood ring, a language only your lover can translate. I could kiss your curved spine, crush your sun-kissed skeleton. Even in deformity—a curved tail as though you broke out of shell, fins stubby and useless—you make the most of life. Wooing with a nod of your head, a feminist at heart. Life's too short to worry about what we can or can't do for another, for ourselves.

REASONS TO CHOOSE THE LIONFISH
AS YOUR LOVER

How uncomplicated we are. Before we become common. Before we inseminate.

AND REASONS NOT TO

Ocean pest. Roll over in bed. Swim in sheets that maul our limbs. Drop mucus-filled egg clusters. Mouth at my back. Terrible fish breath. I am fickle. Can't stay faithful to save my life. Entangled legs. Weightless bodies. We laugh. Our spit pools, spools in coils. Bubbles split the surface.

REASONS TO CHOOSE THE OCTOPUS AS YOUR LOVER

Eight tentacles. A hundred tiny cups to suck. Morphs to camouflage (i.e., your favourite celebrity). Master of disguise (warning: a bit of a player). Savvy; smooth talker who keeps you guessing. Manoeuvres in tight places (has no internal or external skeleton). Only the blue-ringed octopus (his Harley, his soft leather jacket against your cheek) is deadly.

AND REASONS NOT TO

There are dreams of others. Pressed chests together like tight barnacles, the shredded silence of wet open mouths. Gulp sweat and warm night air. Swim in a glittery smear of phosphorescent stars. There is always another imperfect fit; one who eats deep-fried Mars bars and says your thighs are chunky. Who has thirteen lava lamps and struggles to spell words like Christmas and Tucson. Who collects barf bags from airplanes. There is love everywhere, everywhere for the taking.

NOTES AND ACKNOWLEDGMENTS

I am grateful to the literary magazine editors who published earlier versions of these poems. "Oyster" and "Rescue" were shortlisted for Arc's Poem of the Year contest (2008 and 2015). "Intertidal Zones" was published as a limited-edition chapbook with JackPine Press. "Flash Flood," "Only He Knows the Story of His Precious and Particular Life," "Prologue (II)," "Klaus Ricardo," "Dickie Lake 1," "The Summer I Capsized You," and "Dickie Lake 2" were published as a limited-edition chapbook called *Everything Water* with Cactus Press. "Mimic" was published as a chapbook by Leaf Press and won the 2012 bpNichol Chapbook Award. "The Hanged Woman" was shortlisted for the 2008 CBC Literary Awards. My appreciation and gratitude goes to Lisa Johnson and the JackPine Collective, Jim Johnstone and Cactus Press, Ursula Vaira and Leaf Press, and the judges for *Arc*'s Poem of the Year contest in 2008 and 2015, the 2008 CBC Literary Awards, and the 2012 bpNichol Award for their acknowledgment and support of my work.

Much gratitude goes to the Canada Council for the Arts, the BC Arts Council, and the Ontario Arts Council, as well as *ARC* magazine and *Descant* magazine for generous financial assistance while I worked on this collection.

A huge thank you to everyone at BookThug. To Kate Hargreaves for her stunning cover design. To Ruth Zuchter for her copy editing genius. Especially to Jay MillAr and Hazel Millar, two of the kindest and coolest people in the Canadian literary scene. It's not often that a writer gets to publish with their dream publisher. I am honoured and thrilled.

Jim Johnstone, Linda Besner, Calondra Mainhart, and Leah Horlick provided important editorial suggestions on many of these poems in their early drafts, as well as love, support, friendship, and food.

Alex Leslie, this book and my sanity depended deeply on our PHOEM workshops and Q&A play dates. Thank you, sweet friend.

Brecken Hancock, your beautiful and insightful edits were the mini cherries on top of the regular cherry on top of the sundae of awesome that is our friendship. Thank you.

Special thanks to Rachel Rose, Brecken Hancock, and Jim Johnstone for your words.

Thank you to Zachari Logan for generously lending some of your 'Specimens' to collaborate with the chapbook *Intertidal Zones*. Your work inspires my work. I am so lucky to know you.

I could not write poems without my friends and family. You are my rocks.

§

The italicized lines in *The Near-Death Experiences You Inevitably Hear While Learning How to Dive* are taken from the PADI Open Water Diver Manual.

The italicized lines in *Prologue* (II), *Klaus Ricardo,* and *The Summer I Capsized You* are taken from the conversation between Lidia Yuknavitch and Cheryl Strayed in Dear Sugar, *The Rumpus Advice Column #73: I'm Standing Right Next To You.*

The italicized line in *Reasons to Choose the Starfish as Your Lover* is taken from Adam Dickinson's poem "Philosophy Is Going Uphill," printed in *Breathing Fire 2*.

§

"Prologue (I)" is for Edith Gruber and Salvador Lozada, for your hospitality and for providing the home where this book was born. And for Lupita, Enrique, Chava and eventually, Klein Klaus. "The Hanged Woman" is for Klaus Gruber, for passing on your love of road trips. "The Planets Never Align For You" is for Allison Cammer. Your heart is the best measure. "Only He Knows the Story of His Precious and Particular Life" is for the precious Matthew J. Trafford. "Mimic" is for Dennis Hill. The way we mimic. "Oyster" is for Christian Gruber. And for New York. "Klaus Ricardo" is for Edith Gruber and Klaus Lozada, November 23, 2009. "Dickie Lake 1 & 2" are for Linda Besner and Matthew J. Trafford, for retreats past and future. "The Swimmer Vignettes" are for Margaret Gruber, for passing on your love of water. "The Near-Death Experiences You Inevitably Hear While Learning How to Dive" is for Michael Harris, without whom I wouldn't have met my D. "Open Water" is for Anita McCartney, for those first dives together and the photo you took.

Lastly,

Q, my little seahorse. You were in this book from the beginning, I just didn't know it. Since your birth I cannot help myself; every last poem is for you.

T, my little octopus. You began and then arrived at the perfect time to celebrate this book with me. Welcome to the world, Sweetheart.

D, my best man-friend, dive partner and all around love. Remember the seahorse? Xoxo.

ADRIENNE GRUBER is the author of the poetry collection *This is the Nightmare* (2008; shortlisted for the Robert Kroetsch Award for Innovative Poetry) and three chapbooks: *Intertidal Zones* (2014), *Mimic* (2012; winner of a bpNichol Chapbook Award), and *Everything Water* (2011). Her work has appeared in numerous literary magazines, including *Grain, Event, Arc Poetry Magazine, Poetry is Dead,* and *Plentitude.* She has been a finalist for the CBC Literary Awards in poetry, *Descant*'s Winston Collins Best Canadian Poem Contest, and twice for *Arc*'s Poem of the Year Contest. Her poem "Gestational Trail" was awarded first prize in *The Antigonish Review*'s Great Blue Heron Poetry Contest in 2015. Gruber lives in Vancouver with her partner Dennis and their two daughters.

COLOPHON

Manufactured as the first edition of *Buoyancy Control* in the spring of 2016 by BookThug. Distributed in Canada by the Literary Press Group: www.lpg.ca. Distributed in the US by Small Press Distribution: www.spdbooks.org. Shop online at www.bookthug.ca.

Cover design by Kate Hargreaves
Text by Jay MillAr
Copy edited by Ruth Zuchter